Meditations on Eucharist

TABLE

BREAD

and

CUP

SELECTIONS FROM ASSEMBLY

edited by Nathan Mitchell

ALL THE MATERIAL IN THIS VOLUME
ORIGINALLY APPEARED IN *ASSEMBLY*,
A NEWSLETTER PUBLISHED BY THE NOTRE
DAME CENTER FOR PASTORAL LITURGY.
ART WORK TAKEN FROM *ASSEMBLY* BY
JANE PITZ. SUBSCRIPTIONS TO *ASSEMBLY*
MAY BE ORDERED BY CONTACTING
LITURGY TRAINING PUBLICATIONS,
1800 NORTH HERMITAGE AVENUE,
CHICAGO, IL 60622-1101.

CONTENTS

ON THE TABLE, AT THE TABLE

*I*n a dazzling apostrophe found toward the end of Book VII of his *Confessions,*
St. Augustine exclaims,

> *Your brightness bore down relentlessly on me, shimmering, shaking my feeble*
> *gaze 'till I trembled with terror and love. I found myself wandering far away from you*
> *in the land of unlikeness—until, suddenly, I heard you cry: "I am food for grownups;*
> *grow and you will feed on me. You will not change me into yourself, like the ordinary*
> *food your flesh feeds upon; no, you will be changed into me!"*

[Confessions, VII.16; My translation]

*E*ucharist, Augustine suggests in this startling passage, subverts even the most fundamental
human functions—like eating and drinking. Ordinarily our bodies metabolize whatever we
consume, assimilating it to our own flesh, transforming it into ourselves. Not so at the table of
Christ. There, the food and drink that lie *on* the table *turn* the tables, transforming us into the very
Body and Blood we consume. For Christ has a far better right to be called food and drink than
bread and wine do.

*S*ixteen centuries after Augustine's ecstatic celebration of Christ's eucharistic gift, Benedictine
Father Aidan Kavanagh wrote,

> The eucharist is a rite that intensifies change and causes it to take place continually
> according to the same pattern of Jesus' own change from death to a life no one had ever
> lived before. We break the bread of his body, we pour out the cup of his blood in sacri-
> fice. Paul VI and Mrs. Murphy can know this; kings and paupers can know it; professors
> and freshmen can know it. It isn't hard for lots to know, but it is supremely difficult to
> live without sham or full-scale retreat. Baptism and eucharist are really one corporate

person dying and rising. That is a lot to load onto simple things like water and oil, bread and wine. But they never complain. They have never sinned either. They are faithful and close to God in their original innocence, therefore, to a degree that staggers one's imagination. To become like them is what he came to show us. They are superb as God meant us to be. To get that way is a passion for us who have fallen, as it were, into reason.

[Aidan Kavanagh, *"Initiation: Baptism and Confirmation"*, *Worship* 46 (1972): 270]

Superb, as God meant us to be. Father Aidan's phrase could readily stand as an epigraph for this collection of meditations on eucharist drawn from the pages of *Assembly*. The conversion to which Christ's table calls us is not an onerous, plodding path toward a meager scrap of bread and sip of wine; it is a joyful procession (like the communion rite itself), where the assembly gathered *at* the table sings and acclaims, receives and becomes the very food and drink that lie *on* the table—the holy Body of Christ, member for member.

*N*o sacrament, of course, exists in a liturgical or theological vacuum; none exists in isolation. Each sacrament belongs to a larger network, a system whose components interact and overlap. Every sacrament "comments" upon every other—and upon the system as a whole. That is why it is preferable to imagine the sacramental system as a living, breathing organism rather than as a collection of disjunct, "separate but equal" (meaning, of course, separate but *un*equal) rites. That is also why, as Father Aidan suggests, baptism cannot be understood, *sacramentally,* apart from eucharist—nor eucharist apart from baptism. The goal of this system is always the same: to make us "superb, as God meant us to be," as superb as innocent oil and water, bread and wine.

*S*acraments also belong to systems larger than the ecclesial one; they belong as well to those

networks we call "language" and "culture." But here, perspective is especially important. We often imagine that it is the function of human practices and human sciences (the anthropology of a meal, for example) to "explain" sacrament. But of course nothing could be further from the truth. If the anthropology of a meal "explained" eucharist, then we could simply let cultural custom and social convention determine who sits down with whom, who eats what with whom. We could "fence" our tables the way restaurants sometimes do—keeping out the "undesirables," denying them service. But such a table would not be Christ's table. For anthropology cannot explain eucharist; *rather, eucharist "explains" the anthropology of a meal.* True, dining remains a cultural custom, a familiar social convention—but eucharist is neither "language of our present" nor "language of our past;" it is the language of our *future* that redefines our deeds at table as answerable actions, *accountable* actions. At table with Christ, we can no longer drive a wedge between ethics and eucharist, economics and eucharist. At eucharist, the future (God's reign or kingdom; God's eschatological banquet; the Supper of the Lamb) pitches its tent among us, takes possession of us. As Marcel Proust once said, "Sometimes the future lives in us without our knowing it!"

*S*o a church that doesn't feed the poor cannot, as paragraph 1397 of the *Catechism of the Catholic Church* explains, authentically or fruitfully celebrate the eucharist. What we do at a table isn't merely a "liturgical act"; it is an ethical and economic challenge. We gather at table not so much to celebrate our "Catholic identity" as to become what Jesus was and remains—bread broken, wine poured out for the life of the world.

*M*ay these meditations shimmer with God's brightness; may they cause your heart to shake not only with joy, but with challenging conviction. May you leave them refreshed—and disturbed.

—Nathan Michell, Editor
Lent and Easter in the Jubilee Year 2000

THE ASSEMBLY OF A HOLY PEOPLE

a people
>   called to offer God
>   the prayers of the entire human family,

a people
>   giving thanks in Christ
>   for the mystery of salvation
>   by offering his sacrifice . . .

a people
>   growing together in unity . . .

a people
>   holy in their origin.

General Instruction of the Roman Missal [GIRM 4-5]

1

THE ASSEMBLY

is a radically inclusive body.

It embraces all the baptized—
  the people and their ministers,
  women and men,
  children and adults,
  rich and poor,
  "somebodies" and "nobodies,"
  familiar friends
  and struggling strangers,
  the ordained and the non-ordained.

The sublime sacrament
of the whole church . . .
                    [SC 5]

*T*he one who presides at the eucharist
  (whether presbyter, bishop or pope)
  is always, first, a member of *the assembly*,
  called with the rest of the congregation
  to deeds of mercy, love and justice
  for the life of the world.
  Indeed,
the eucharist creates the church precisely because it celebrates
the paschal mystery.
For as *Sacrosanctum Concilium* puts it,
      From the side of Christ
      as he slept upon the cross . . . there issued forth
      the sublime sacrament of the whole church.

Nathan Mitchell, *The Assembly as Minister,* Editorial, 25.2 [1999]

Through his greeting, the priest declares to the assembled community that the Lord is present. [GIRM 28]

𝒯he liturgical assembly is not another *audience*, [GIRM 28] and the act of assembling is not just another process of arriving and taking places. The liturgy is an act of the Church—the Church as realized in a local congregation—which is the Body of Christ.

ASSEMBLY

𝒯hus, this assembled people is itself the primary sacrament of Christ, the outward and visible sign of the presence of Christ in and to the world, the medium of his own continuing mediatorship for the glorification of God and the sanctification of the human race.

𝒯hus we may speak of the assembly as the primary and indispensable source of the sacramentality of the sacraments. . . .

𝒯hey are acts of the church; they are acts of Christ. Consequently, the process by which people gather for Mass and enter into the rite is actually the process of *people-becoming-sacrament*.

Mark Searle, *Collecting and Recollecting*, 11.1 [1984]

*The places for the
faithful should be
arranged with care
so that the people are
able to take their rightful
part in the celebration
visually and mentally.*
[GIRM 273]

WHO IS THE ASSEMBLY?

*C*learly, the challenge before us is one of inclusion. . . .
How do we allow the story of love incarnate
to be shared in our liturgical assemblies among people
who differ because of culture, language, economic class, age,
physical and mental ability, gender and sexual orientation?
A place to start is to heed the prophetic statement
of the African American bishops in their pastoral letter
What We Have Seen and Heard:

*All people should be able to recognize themselves when
Christ is presented, and should be able to experience their
own fulfillment when these mysteries are celebrated.*

Mark Francis, CSV, *Who is the Assembly?*, 25.2 [1999]

Christ is really present to the assembly gathered in his name.

[GIRM 7]

$\mathcal{T}$he work of the assembly—
their responsibility and right by baptism—
is to come together explicitly
to acknowledge God in prayer and praise,
publicly to feast the mystery of salvation
already accomplished by Christ,
to thank and glorify God for this mystery
so that it may be intensified in themselves
and communicated to others for the building up of the church;
in other words, the ministry of the assembly
is to be the church at prayer.

John K. Leonard, *Presiding at Liturgical Prayer*, 14.5 [1988]

CELEBRATION

The celebration of Mass . . .
is for the universal and the local church,
as well as for each person, the center of the whole Christian life.

[GIRM 1]

$\mathcal{C}$elebration is necessarily linked to one's experience.

Two things are implied.

First, celebration means to own, accept, acknowledge and embrace
one's experience in its totality. . . .

(continued)

*C*elebration
means acknowledging and proclaiming the experience as genuinely mine. . . .
Liturgy does not invite hypocrites to play church
for an hour or a Pentecost,
but urges ever more intense penetration of daily paschal life
where wonder endures,
even in the contextual holocaust of radical treachery.

*S*o the second implication of celebration
is the discovery that one's experience, in fact,
does disclose the presence of a power
that is stronger than the power of death,
more beautiful than the outrages of ugliness. . . .
Celebration proclaims that, in one's experience,
    life overcomes death,
    light overcomes darkness,
    freedom overcomes slavery.
Celebration does not indulge in the pretension
that evil, death, darknesss or slavery are not real.
Celebration does not make us blind to pain
or deaf to the howlings of anguish.
Celebration *sees wonders* in the midst of suffering. . . .

    *T*he reign of God
    which arrives in the coming of Jesus Christ
    is the era of Cana,
    the time when the water of human experience,
    in its whole range of goodness and evil,
    is made into the new wine of divinity, a new creation.
    In this era of Cana, death is transformed into life,
    and all humanity rises with Christ.

John Gallen, SJ, *Celebrating the Season*, 20.1 [1994]

COMMAND

At whose command we celebrate this eucharist . . . [EP III]

His to command, ours to obey
He obedient unto death, we obeying unto life
His to lead, ours to follow
His to suffer, ours to find hope in suffering
His to hunger and thirst, ours to feast in his kingdom
His to die, ours to trample on death

His to descend into hell, ours to exult with his saints
His to yield up his spirit, ours to receive it
His to be sown in the cold earth,
    ours to reap the harvest of salvation
His to glorify the Father, ours to bear witness to his glory
His to redeem, ours to give thanks for redemption
His to command, ours to obey.

Mark Searle, *Praying the Liturgy* 11.4 [1985]

FASTING

$\mathcal{F}$asting brings new wholeness to our relationships.
Self-preservation and self-enhancement—
often unconsciously at work—
may become powerful, destructive tools
of self-advancement at the expense of others.
How arduous to listen without being engaged in our own agendas!
How difficult to feel neglected or ridiculed—and not to retaliate!
How tempting to show our colleagues how much we really know!
How easy to keep our children from being who they are
because we want them to fill up what is lacking in our own lives!

Not eating may seem far removed from these episodes,
but the purifying, healing effects of fasting
can reach even into the realm of human interaction.

Real love is possible only in one who lets go of self-delusion
and comes into possession of the deepest self.
The one who fasts has set out on this journey of separation
and becomes more and more free to love.
Perhaps that is why, for so many centuries,
Christians came fasting to the eucharistic table.

Barbara Searle, *Sacrifice and Fasting*, 10.4 [1984]; reprinted 23.1 [1997]

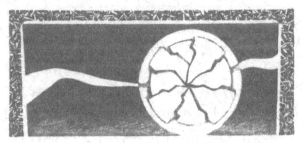

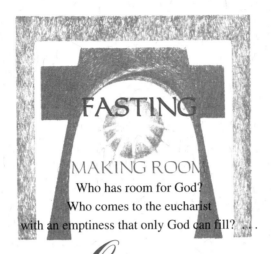

FASTING

MAKING ROOM

Who has room for God?
Who comes to the eucharist
with an emptiness that only God can fill? . . . .

*O*nce upon a time,
people used to fast before coming to worship.
By the time this spiritual discipline
had passed out of our experience,
it had devolved
into a meaningless exercise in clock-watching.

*A*lthough I am not recommending a return
to these often *mindless* practices,
there is something to be said for coming to the banquet table hungry—
hungering both physically and spiritually.

*P*hysical hunger
that reminds us ultimately of our deep spiritual hunger
for communion with each other and with God
can be a powerful religious experience.

Julie Upton, RSM, *Real Absence*, 23.3 [1997]

FLESH

Now he is seen as one like us . . .
[Christmas Preface II]

Whoever eats my flesh
and drinks my blood
will live in me . . .
[John 6.57; Communion Antiphon for Corpus Christi]

The flesh is the hinge on which salvation depends.
When the soul is dedicated to God,
it is the flesh which actually makes it capable of such dedication.
For surely the flesh is washed that the soul may be cleansed.
The flesh is anointed that the soul may be consecrated.
The flesh is sealed that the soul may be fortified.
The flesh is overshadowed by the imposition of hands
that the soul may be illumined by the Spirit.
The flesh feeds on the body and blood of Christ
that the soul may fatten on God.

Tertullian, *On the Resurrection of the Flesh*, C. 8; 19.4 [1993]

10

Through Christ you give us
all these gifts.
You fill them with life and goodness.
You bless them and make them holy. [EP I]

Let your Spirit come upon these gifts to make them holy. [EP II]

*M*inutes before
    this bread, this cup,
        held tightly
    in the couple's gnarled
    and work-worn fingers,

*S*he walks down the aisle
    this uncomfortable girl-child
    awkward
    in the first anguishing throes
    of adolescent bewilderment.
    Vulnerable, alone
    in this assembly of many.

    You fill her with life and goodness,
    you bless her and make her holy.

A toddler awakes
    and lifts his sleepy head
    longing for home and toys,
    lunch and play.
    His weary parents
    breathe a silent prayer
    for strength and patience
    as the presider intones

    You fill them with life and goodness,
    you bless them and make them holy.

*T*his bread, this cup
    these hearts, these lives,
    held as one
    through Christ our Lord,
    who gives us all these gifts—
    who blesses them and makes them holy.

Teresa Ball, *Praying the Liturgy*, 11.4 [1985]

the fruit of the vine
and work of human hands:

You fill them
with life and goodness,
you bless them
and make them holy.

It is fitting for the faithful's participation to be expressed
by their presenting both the bread and wine for the celebration of
the eucharist and other gifts to meet the needs of the church and of
the poor. [GIRM 101]

*C*hristians pray in many ways:
> We mark the hours of the day with psalms.
> We bring succor to the sick.
> We gather at table at home.

GIFT

*B*ut the eucharist alone
embodies an action of offering.
You can receive communion at a communion service,
but if you aspire to celebrate eucharist,
you come with gifts for the poor.

*T*he General Instruction of the Roman Missal [49] calls for
the reception of money or other gifts for the church or the poor
at the time when the bread and wine are brought to the altar.
Astoundingly, the bread and wine
—the elements most central to the eucharist we celebrate—
come to the altar accompanied by offerings for the poor.

*E*ucharist is thanksgiving; eucharist is communion;
and eucharist is charity.

Paul Turner, *Gifts for the Poor*, 24.5 [1998]

INCENSE

*The priest goes up to the altar and kisses it. If incense is used,
he incenses the altar while circling it.* [GIRM 85]

*F*ew people appreciate the evocative and musical power of
incense the way Eastern Christians do.
The sight, smell and sound of the censer are essential
not only in the preparations and processions of the Divine Liturgy
but are central features at the *incense hours*
of Morning and Evening Prayer each day [Exodus 30.7-8, 34-38].
The accompanying chants and prayers make it clear
that this *outpouring of unwitholding love*
is to usher worshipers into the Beauty of the Divine Presence:
the Burning Bush [Exodus 3], the smoke-filled Temple [Isaiah 6.4],
where the prayers of uplifted hands rise like incense [Psalm 141.2],
where God's plan of liberation was revealed to Zachariah
[Luke 1.9-11], and the smoke of the spices ascends before the face of
God [Revelation 8.3-4].

What is this sweet-smelling offering?
For Christians, it is Christ Jesus himself,
the golden altar of incense and the ark of the covenant [Hebrews 9.4],
who lifted his arms in the once-and-for-all acceptable sacrifice
and presented the sweet fragrance of his entire self [Psalm 40.7-8],
the very incarnation of Unwitholding Love.

John K. Leonard, *Holy Smoke: The Use of Incense in Worship*, 24.4 [1998]

INTERCESSION

In the general intercessions . . . the people,
exercising their priestly function, intercede for all humanity. [GIRM 45]

Petitions will be offered for the church, for civil authorities,
for those oppressed by various needs, for all people,
and for the salvation of the world. [GIRM 45]

*T*he work of intercession is not self-initiated.
Its placement at the conclusion of the Liturgy of the Word
indicates its nature as response. . . .
To make intercession in the liturgy
is to place before God in the public gathering
the universal concerns that burden the human family.

*I*t is to pray with an expanded consciousness,
taking one's cue from the model prayer
that the Lord himself taught us:
Thy kingdom come . . . thy will be done . . . give us daily bread . . .
To petition is not to bargain with God,
to change God's mind or alter God's plans.
The favors we request are, on the one hand,
our own feeble attempt to acknowledge what is yet wanting,
to cry out for what needs to be healed.
On the other hand, the petitions are a way of declaring publicly
that what we most need
we are incapable of acquiring for ourselves.

Eleanor Bernstein, CSJ, *Enabling Intercession*, 13.1 [1986]

INTRODUCTORY RITES

*The purpose of these rites is that the faithful coming together
take on the form of a community and prepare themselves
to listen to God's word and celebrate the eucharist.* [GIRM 24]

*In the name of the Father,
and of the Son,
and of the Holy Spirit.*

GREETING

*T*he introductory rites are intended to foster that process
whereby we become aware of who we are and what we are about
as a celebrating assembly of faithful people.
They prepare us to *celebrate these sacred mysteries,*
to enter into that mysterious network of relationships
we call *Father, Son and Spirit.*

*T*hey lead us into a state of being consciously *in Christ,*
by surrendering to the suffusing presence of the Spirit,
so as to stand as a Body/people before the throne
of the One Jesus called *Abba.*

*I*n that network of relationships the *sacrum commercium,*
the *holy intercourse* of the liturgy, unfolds in Word and Sacrament,
but it will largely pass us by if the introductory rites
have not introduced us once again to this mysterious state.

Mark Searle, *Collecting and Recollecting,* 11.1 [1984]

LIGHT

A sign of reverence and festivity . . . [GIRM 269]

In every age and culture,
   artists have used light
   as an image of the divine presence.

   The artists who wrote the gospels
   were adept at this skill
   of turning the psychic and mythic power of fire and light
   toward Christ.
   We are not surprised to read
   that he is

> *the light of all people* [John 1],
> *the light of the world* [John 8],
> *a light for the Gentiles* [Luke 2], and
> *a light from heaven* [Acts 22].

The liturgy is filled with canticles and hymns to the light,
prayers for enlightenment
and softly burning candles that mark the precincts of worship
more modestly than Solomon's towering lampstands.
We present candles to the newly baptized
and exhort them to let their light shine before others [Matthew 5].
We bless candles at Candlemas
and pray for God's protection as candles rest on our throats.

Samuel Torvend, *Holy Presence*, 24.4 [1998]

Holy Light, O Blessed Night
God says again, *Let there be light.*
Holy Light, Most Blessed Light
Christ our Light. Thanks be to God!
O darkest night, most deadly night?
NO! Deadly for death is this night!

Holy Light, Most Blessed Light
Darkness abounds, all is night
But darkness dims in your Holy Light
Radiance so great, yea,
Even darkness is bright!

Holy Light, O Living Light
Your creatures share creating light!
Holy Light, Most Blessed Light
God's promise to make all right:
Your son, born on another night!

Holy Light, O Burning Light
Flaming bush before Moses'sight!
Holy Light, O Guiding Light
leading your people through their plight!
Holy Light, O come this night
Magi chase your guiding star's light!
Holy Light, shine on this boy
Grow him in age, wisdom and might!

A new and radiant vision of your glory . . .
[Christmas Preface I]

Holy Light, O Kindly Light
A man born blind seeks his sight.
Holy Light, in darkest night
In our blindness we seek your Light.

Holy Light, O Christ Our Light
Grace abounds, all is right.
Christ, our Way, our Truth, our Life,
Guide us, standing in this holy light.

Kurt Stasiak, OSB, *Standing in This Holy Light,* 24.4 [1998]

18

LOVE (EUCHARIST)

He always loved those who were his own in the world . . . [EP IV]

He showed the depth of his love . . . [EP IV]

All love that ever was, that ever shall be
finds its root, its wellspring, here:
for love is of God
and God is love.
Look upon the broken bread,
the cup of bitterness and joy,
and know your God.
Know the depths of God
in the wounded side
in the pierced heart
of Christ.
Knowing the depths of God beyond all knowing,
slake your thirst of his fullness.

Mark Searle, *Praying the Liturgy*, 11.4 [1985]

MINISTRY

*P*aul's work shows ministry arising
from within the messy experience of conversion and faith.
Ministry is the "outflow" of "seeing the Lord,"
of being rudely shaken and utterly changed
by the fierce impact of God's grace
breaking out uncontrollably in human life.
Thus, the notion that one can be *prepared* or *presented* for ministry
—the way a debutante is presented to society—
is completely foreign to Paul's perception of ministerial vocation.

*B*oasting of his own weakness,
unimpressive appearance,
and poor skills in public speaking,
Paul claimed that his *status* resulted
from the fact that he was a wreck—
and that human wreckage
was the surest sign of God's power
doing for him what he could never do for himself.

*P*aul's *status* as a minister
celebrated grace, not the self,
with its contrived resume of achievements.
And grace, for Paul, was God's self-bestowal
pouring into life on its own terms,
pouring torrentially, exuberantly,
into vessels so fragile they seemed to break up and disappear.

> *All in the assembly gathered for Mass
> have an individual right and duty
> to contribute their participation
> in ways differing
> according to the diversity of their order
> and liturgical function.
> In carrying out this function,
> all, whether ministers or laypersons,
> should do all and only those parts
> that belong to them.*
> [GIRM 58]
>
> *They are to shun any appearance
> of individualism or divison . . .* [GIRM 62]

*S*elf-loss and surrender are thus the experiences
to which Paul attached the power and permanence of ministry.
Such surrender cannot be transmitted through a rite,
and the status it brings is the status of one
who has passed through the wringer of conversion.

Nathan Mitchell, *Terms of Attachment,* 16.1 [1989]

20

The faithful should serve the people of God willingly
when asked to perform some particular ministry in the celebration. [GIRM 62]

At the heart of the formation experience of the RCIA
is the retrieval of a baptismal spirituality
that affirms all the baptized as gifted
and called by the Divine
for service of the mission of the reign of God.
No one can be excluded.
In fact, an essential dimension of the initiation covenant
is to actively continue the mission of Jesus (i.e., true discipleship).
This universal call to mission serves as the foundation for all forms
of ministry, including the ordained ministry.

Thomas H. Morris, *The Ministry of the Baptized,* 16.1 [1989]

MINISTRY

A place for all at the table . . .
Baptism gives each of us
a place of honor
at God's table,
on earth and in heaven. . . .

Baptism makes us all equal, all privileged.
When we enter the holy house for worship,
we must leave at the door
whatever our pride makes us hold most dear:
our special claims to honor,
our personal achievements,
our good works.
Such pride and self-importance have no place
in those who could never earn the priceless gift
that God lavishes upon us in the body of Christ;
they will only get in the way of our ministry
to the members of that body.

Michael Kwatera, OSB, *Chosen Race, Royal Priesthood, Holy People,* 25.2 [1999]

For you, with you . . .
When I am frightened by what I am *for* you,
then I am consoled by *what* I am with you.
For you, I am a bishop;
with you, I am a Christian.
The first is an office, the second a grace;
the first is dangerous,
the second brings salvation.

Augustine, Sermon 340 cited in *Lumen Gentium* 32;
The Assembly as Minister, Editorial, 25.2 [1999]

MUSIC

St. Augustine says rightly, "To sing belongs to lovers." [GIRM 19]

One who sings well prays twice. [GIRM 19]

Music's duty is clear and twofold—
create a mode that expresses the liturgy with its ritual action and
create a mood that reflects the ambience the liturgy requires. . . .
This is especially true with the sacraments that deal
with pastoral care.

The anointings with the touch of flesh on flesh;
the order of funerals
with its processional scheme of wake, church and gravesite;
the church's embrace of the reconciled—
all utilize ritual texts and acts which are transformed
when they are sung or framed with musical expression.

Musical expressions lend a connectedness to the pastoral rites . . .
which speak of Jesus' consolation, his mercy,
 encouragement, peace — whatever broken humanity needs.
The music seeks to connect all of those qualities to the human gathering
and to heal all the brokenness, to make all things whole and new.

Fred Moleck, *Music at the Service of the Rites,* 15.5 [1989]

O endless ages' Strength,
    creation found a home within your heart.
    You chose to share your life,
    by calling forth all creatures through your Word.

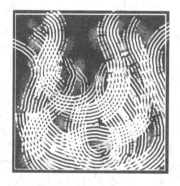

And taking human form,
    your very Word adorned itself with flesh—
    so freeing flesh from anguish, loss and pain.

How wondrous is the love
    that urged the Saving One who frees all things
    to share our human breath
    and live our life.

By breaking bonds of sin,
    the Word freed flesh from anguish, loss and pain.

To Parent, Spirit, Child
    be glory from all creatures low and high,
    whose lives were saved from anguish, loss and pain.

Hildegard of Bingen, *Song of the Creating Word*, 16.5 [1990]

MUSIC

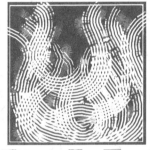

*T*here are times in musical prayer
when the aura and beauty of the moment
surpasses the meaning of the text itself,
allowing for an intense experience of contemplation.

This is not to undermine the importance of the prayer text,
nor the ministerial function which music has
in supporting the word of the liturgy.
Yet a fully catholic understanding of music in worship
must give value to the contemplative dimension of
musical prayer.

Charles Conley, *Musical Participation,* 6.2 [1979]

*S*inging is not something that accompanies worship
(in the way, for instance, that adoring fans
accompany a rock star on a triumphant tour).
Singing is part of the liturgical act itself
(as are prayer, proclamation, listening,
silence, movement, eating and drinking, etc.).
If there is no music at our worship,
then this does not mean that the event
is merely *less solemn* or *less beautiful*—

it means that we have forgotten how to do
an essential part of the liturgical act. . . .
There are some tasks
—and the assembly's worship is one of these—
that can't be done except in song.

Nathan Mitchell, *The Song of Creation: Liturgy and Music,*
Editorial, 16.5 [1990]

*A*ll of God's creatures, assembled for worship,
are ministers of music.
The assembly, presider, deacon, cantor, choir,
instrumentalists, organist and composer are all
called to full, conscious and active participation
when gathered together as people
who have encountered Jesus Christ,
have heard his word, and have responded in faith. . . .

*W*e gather, fully aware of what we are doing,
to express and deepen our faith
while wholeheartedly entering into the celebration,
into the Mystery,

with thoughts, words, songs, ritual gestures—
all deep expressions
of the reality of our love for Christ
and for one another.

Rosemary Hudecheck, *A Place in the Choir,* 16.5 [1990]

MUSIC

MYSTAGOGY

The main setting for mystagogy . . .
is the Sunday Masses of the Easter Season. [RCIA 247]

Searching the heights and depths of mystery . . .

*O*ften *it seems*

> that people don't want to be engaged by mystery,
> but entertained in spite of it.
> There are life experiences, however,
> that plunge us into mystery
> with a suddenness that we are unable to escape.
>> The once amiable Mississippi turns tyrant,
>> the child next door is abducted and brutally murdered,
>> fires burn out of control
>> swallowing up not only homes and lives,
>> but nature's protective sheaving as well,
>> and we stand speechless.

*S*uch is the time for mystagogy.

>> A certain degree of mystagogy should mark all our days
>> and each of our eucharistic celebrations,
>> but it is during the blessed Pentecost, the holy fifty days,
>> when the Church—the company of believers—
>> together tries to fathom yet again
>> the heights and the depths of the paschal mystery.

Julia Upton, RSM, *The Mystagogic Moment,* 20.1 [1994]

MYSTERY

By shedding his blood for us, . . .
Jesus Christ established the paschal mystery.
[Good Friday Opening Prayer]

Let us proclaim the mystery of faith. [EP 1]

Felled grain made bread for hungry crowds,
spilled blood outpoured in covenant cup,
our once lord, Death, held thrall to Life,
the many made one flesh:
O wonderful exchange of love
wrought yet not wrought
until you come
in glory.

Genevieve Glen, OSB, 11.4 [1985]

*W*hat you see on God's altar, you've already observed
    —during the night that has now ended.
    But you've heard nothing about just what it might be,
    or what it might mean,
    or what great thing it might be said to symbolize.
    For what you see is simply bread and a cup—
    this is the information your eyes report.
    But your faith demands far subtler insight—
    the bread is Christ's body, the cup is Christ's blood.
    Faith can grasp the fundamentals quickly, succinctly,
    yet it hungers for a fuller account of the matter.
    As the prophet says,
    Unless you believe, you will not understand.
    [Isaiah 7.9; Septuagint]
    So you can say to me,
    You urged us to believe—now explain, so we can understand.

*I*nside each of you, thoughts like these are rising:

    *O*ur Lord Jesus Christ—we know the source of his flesh;
    he took it from the virgin Mary.
    Like any infant, he was nursed and nourished;
    he grew; became a youngster;
    suffered persecution from his own people.
    To the wood he was nailed; on the wood he died;
    from the wood, his body was taken down and buried.
    On the third day (as he willed) he rose;
    he ascended bodily into heaven—
    whence he will come to judge the living and the dead.
    There he dwells even now, seated at God's right.
    So how can bread be his body? And what about the cup—
    how can it (or what it contains) be his blood?

My friends, these realities are called sacraments
　　　　because in them one thing is seen, while another is grasped.
　　　　What is seen is a mere physical likeness;
　　　　what is grasped bears spiritual fruit.

So now, if you want to understand the body of Christ,
　　　　listen to the Apostle Paul speaking to the faithful:

You are the body of Christ, member for member. [1 Corinthians 12.27]
　　　　If you, therefore, are Christ's body and members,
　　　　it is your own mystery that is placed on the Lord's table!
　　　　It is your own mystery that you are receiving!
　　　　You are saying *"Amen"* to what you are—
　　　　your response is a personal signature, affirming your faith.
　　　　When you hear *"The body of Christ"*—you reply *"Amen"*.
　　　　Be a member of Christ's body, then,
　　　　so that your *Amen* may ring true!
　　　　But what role does the bread play?
　　　　We have no theory of our own to propose here;
　　　　listen, instead, to what Paul says about this sacrament:

The bread is one, and we, though many, are one body. [1 Corinthians 10.17]
　　　　Understand and rejoice—unity, truth, faithfulness, love.
　　　　One bread, he says. What is this one bread?
　　　　Is it not the *one body*, formed from many?
　　　　Remember: bread doesn't come from a single grain,
　　　　but from many.
　　　　When you received exorcism, you were *ground.*
　　　　When you were baptized, you were *leavened.*
　　　　When you received the fire of the Holy Spirit,
　　　　you were *baked.*
　　　　Be what you see; receive what you are.
　　　　This is what Paul is saying about the bread.

So too, what we are to understand about the cup
　　　　is similar and requires little explanation.
　　　　In the visible object of bread, many grains
　　　　are gathered into one—just as the faithful (so Scripture says)
　　　　form *a single heart and mind in God.* [Acts 4.32]

And thus it is with the wine.

*R*emember, friends, how wine is made—
individual grapes hang together in a bunch,
but the juice from them all is
mingled to become a single brew.
This is the image chosen by Christ our Lord
to show how, at his own table,
the mystery of our unity and peace
is solemnly consecrated.

*A*ll who fail to keep the bond of peace
after entering this mystery
receive not a sacrament that benefits them,
but an indictment that condemns them.

*S*o let us give God our sincere and deepest gratitude—
and, as far as human weakness will permit,
let us turn to the Lord with pure hearts.
With all our strength,
let us seek God's singular mercy,
for then the Divine Goodness
will surely hear our prayers.
God's power will drive the Evil One
from our acts and thoughts;
it will deepen our faith, govern our minds,
grant us holy thoughts, and lead us, finally,
to share the divine happiness
through God's own son Jesus Christ. Amen!

A homily by Saint Augustine
translated by Nathan Mitchell
from the Latin text in J. P. Migne, *Patrologia Latina*
38.1246-1248; 23.2 [1997]

MYSTERY

MYSTERY AND MANNERS

*I*n public prayer and worship, the church makes its identity known:
it tells the world who it is by doing what it does best—
inviting the hurt and hungry, the least and littlest,
to that bountiful Supper of the Lamb
where the oppressive old order collapses,
pain and mourning cease, tears are wiped away,
and death is no more [Revelation 21.4].

*T*he liturgical assembly is that place—or better, that activity—
by which we entrust our deepest beliefs, meanings and values
to the care of human practices. . . .
Human practices, the stuff of creation.

*L*iturgy is corporate ritual activity
that shows us
how the holy is revealed in the human,
the divine in the daily,
mystery in manners.

Nathan Mitchell, *The Assembly as Minister*, Editorial, 25.2 [1999]

PARTICIPATION

The celebration . . . brings about in the faithful
a participation in body and spirit
that is conscious, active, full,
and motivated
by faith, hope and charity.
The Church desires this kind of
participation,
the nature of the celebration
demands it,
and for the Christian people it
is a right and duty
they have by reason of their
baptism. [GIRM 3]

Full participation

does not relate to quantity as much as to quality.
Participation is not necessarily "full" when the
entire community does everything;
in fact, the opposite may obtain.
A blurring of ministries in the community
can hinder fullness of participation.
Sharing in the liturgical celebration is full
insofar as the community fully expresses its new life
in Christ Jesus, each member
expressing his or her gift in an appropriate way.

$\mathcal{E}$ach ministry,
exercised for the benefit of the entire assembly,
gives full expression to the praise of the assembly.

For one to be chosen as reader
implies necessarily that others are active listeners,
opening their hearts to the living Word of God.
For another to lead the community in song
implies that those gathered in prayer
are led in making a joyful song to the Lord.
For others to offer the eucharistic bread and cup
means that there are those
who approach the holy table to accept.

$\mathcal{T}$hrough these mutual ministries
the shared life of the assembly,
made full through the sacrificial life
and death of Jesus,
is expressed.

$\mathcal{W}$e are a people who receive as well as offer;
we are a community who accept as well as give;
we are an assembly filled with the bounty of God's gifts.

John Melloh, SM, *Participation Revisited*, 6.2 [1979]

POSTURE

Uniformity in standing, kneeling, or sitting . . . is a sign of the community and the unity of the assembly. [GIRM 20]

*T*he *General Instruction of the Roman Missal* [54] calls the eucharistic prayer the *center and summit* of the entire celebration.

*W*hile this might be true in a theological sense, it is certainly far from the case in any observable way. . . . One can say theoretically that the eucharistic prayer is the prayer of the whole church, but that theory is contradicted by the bodily posture of worshippers.

*I*nviting all the members of an assembly to stand during the eucharistic prayer expresses a much different theology from having them kneel.

To kneel reverently and prayerfully is to emphasize the sacred nature of what is happening at the altar and, implicitly at least, to recognize that the priest is doing something that the rest of the assembly is not.

To stand, on the other hand, implies that all members of the assembly are actively engaged in making thanksgiving, even if only one voice predominates in the prayer. The prayer would be much more engaged and engaging if people were invited to lift up their hands in prayer not only during the Lord's Prayer but during the eucharistic prayer itself. The *orans* position need not be emblematic of charismatic Christians alone. It embodies an attitude of openness and vulnerability to God and to one another.

John Baldovin, SJ, *Caro Cardo Salutis*, 19.4 [1993]

As we wait in joyful hope . . . [Our Father, embolism]

*W*e who await God's coming
   are invited in the scriptures
   to adopt postures of hope.

> *Stand up and raise your heads,*
> *because your redemption*
> *is drawing near.* [Luke 21.28]

*W*e are not to hide as students do in a classroom when they don't have an answer
         and don't want to be called on. We have the answer. The answer
            comes finally in the clouds—*you will see the Son of Man*
               coming in a cloud with power and great glory [Luke
                  21.27).

*A*dvent trains us in these postures of hope and in
   the mental states which should go along with them.
   As we are standing up, we are to dream of lions and
   lambs peacefully together.
   As advent dreamers, we are to nurture visions,
      images of hope—we are to be a community of hope.
      . . .We need to pray in order to keep standing.
   Prayer keeps us open to hope
      and open to the possible.
   Prayer is the antidote
      to the world's heaviness and despair.
         We need to practice our posture of standing together
and looking to the One who is to come.

Raymond Studzinski, OSB, *The Hope of God's Coming,* 19.5 [1993]

PRAYER

Let us pray for the coming of the kingdom as Jesus taught us. [Our Father, introduction]

*P*articipation requires imagination as well as intellect,
     the unconscious as well as the conscious,
       passive as well as active involvement. . . .
How do we pray the liturgy now in the midst of so many words?
How do we engage the contemplative, non-rational, non-verbal side
of ourselves when we are so geared to hearing words
as bearers of information?
How do we *see* the images of the liturgy
and let ourselves be carried to the place
where they yield their silent meaning?

Barbara Schmich, *Praying the Liturgy*, Editorial, 11.4 [1985]

*I*maginative praying demands a level of comfort
with the kind of language the eucharistic prayer requires.
As the great hymn of praise and thanksgiving,
it must be lyrical in quality
if it is to release religious sentiments in the hearts of its hearers.
It must also make the best use of poetic images
in the service of fatih.
Some words and phrases do not make literal sense,
but literal logic is not always the best vehicle for expressing meaning.
In the realm of mystery,
where we are ultimately dealing with the unknowable,
it is perhaps best not to pretend
that we can make declarative statements.

Barbara Schmich, *Praying the Liturgy*, Editorial, 11.4 [1985]

PRAYER

*W*hile I pray better in private,
I definitely celebrate better in public,
and that is what the banquet is for.
Yes, I have found God, and with that discovery
comes the need—the compulsion even—to share God. . . .

*W*e all live braided lives,
and even within the spiritual plait
there are strands of both public and private prayer.
The mystery of faith
requires that the faithful believe in it,
that they celebrate it,
and that they live it in a vital and personal relationship
with the living and true God. [Catechism of the Catholic Church 2558]

*T*he celebration is liturgy; the relationship is prayer.
In the public prayer we give outward expression
to the internal reality that is our life in and with God,
in whom each of us lives and moves and has our being.

Julia Upton, RSM, *Prayer: Personal and Public,* 21.1 [1995]

PRESENCE

Christ is really present to the assembly gathered in his name;
he is present in the person of the minister, in his own word,
and . . . under the eucharistic elements. [GIRM 7]

CHRIST'S PRESENCE IN THE ASSEMBLY

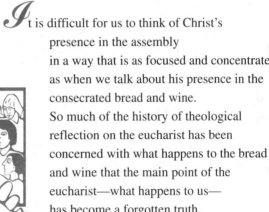

*I*t is difficult for us to think of Christ's
presence in the assembly
in a way that is as focused and concentrated
as when we talk about his presence in the
consecrated bread and wine.
So much of the history of theological
reflection on the eucharist has been
concerned with what happens to the bread
and wine that the main point of the
eucharist—what happens to us—
has become a forgotten truth.

*B*ut surely what happens to us in the
celebration of the eucharist
must be the point of it all.

*C*hrist is present in the bread and wine
not simply to be there
as a chair is *there* in a room,
but to be there personally as with an
individual I/we encounter. . . .

It is much easier to affirm
the *real* presence of Christ
in the consecrated bread and wine
than in the assembly of the faithful.

𝓑read and wine are *out there*.
  They can be defined and analyzed.
  They are different from us and—on one level at least—
  their being the body and blood of Christ do not necessarily
  demand much from us, except an affirmation of faith.
  But if that were all there were to it,
  the eucharist would merely remain
  an interesting aspect of our faith.

𝓘t is, however,
      much more than interesting.
      The eucharist is a challenge
      (paraphrasing St. Augustine)
      to become what we eat, to see ourselves
      laid out on the holy table,
      in other words to be transformed into Christ.

John Baldovin, SJ, *Real Presence: Christ in the Assembly*, 15.2 [1988]

40

EMBODIED PRESENCE

*P*oetry, it has been said, is *memorable speech,*
speech that doesn't merely describe or talk about
but reveals by creating shared experience between
poet and reader.

All poetry thus points to presence—
real, personal and potent.
Poems, writes Donald Hall,
are pleasure first:
bodily pleasure,
a deliciousness of the senses.

Mostly, poems end by saying something (even the unsayable),
but they start as the body's joy, like making love."
[*Poetry: The Unsayable Said* (Port Townsend, WA: Copper Canyon Press, 1993), 2]

*W*e humans cannot imagine presence
apart from our bodies
any more than we can imagine poetry apart from pleasure, . . .

*I*t is no accident that the central symbol of divine
presence in Catholic tradition is a communion of our bodies
with the Body—
Christ offered to us as bread, solace and delight
for our senses,
a boon for our blood, bone and breath. . . .

*F*or Christians,
presence is always an embodied, dynamic, plural reality—
a new way of being alive in a community of persons.
God's presence to us—and our presence to God—
does not dissolve our distinctive identities.
Our destiny is not to merge, in some blind and impersonal way,
with the cosmos.
Rather, as embodied persons we meet a personal God
who calls us to personalize the world.
God's revelation in Christ has forever turned the tables.
No longer does the universe measure us; we measure the universe.
Human beings, in all their grace and grandeur,
failure and fallenness,
are the fulfillment the world seeks—not the other way around.

Nathan Mitchell, *Real Presences*, Editorial, 23.3 [1997]

The power of the Holy Spirit
and the Word of Christ
transform the elements of bread and wine
into the body and blood of the Lord
through the prayer of the church.
This is *real presence*
because it is presence in the fullest sense:
it is the fullest self-giving of Christ to the church;
it is the *totus Christus*—the whole Christ crucified and risen,
body and blood, soul and divinity, head and members.

Yet the full meaning of this real presence is understood . . .
by recognizing the significance of the elements chosen by Christ,
those of food and drink.
In eating and drinking, unity occurs.
What is consumed becomes part of the person,
but also the person becomes more of what is consumed—
you are what you eat. . . .
Christ's real presence is given in the context of food
because food is fraught with the meanings of presence:
self-giving, nurturing, uniting in fellowship.
It is indeed *holy communion.*

*I*n this meal,
    the species of bread and wine are integrated into our bodies,
    transformed into part of us;
    but far more significantly, the members of the church
    are integrated into the reality received,
    are transformed into the Body of Christ,
    so that the words of Paul ring true:
    It is no longer I who live, but Christ who lives in me. [Galatians 2.20]

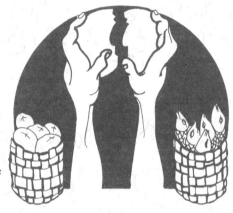

*S*till, . . . there is yet an aspect of presence
that is as essential to eucharist
as it is to all religious experience
if it is to come to its divine purpose and end.
This presence is the human response—it is a responsive presence.
The presence of the church:
    a self-giving and self-disclosure to God,
    the acceptance of God into our lives,
completes the intention of God in the experience of *real presence.*

*I*n traditional theological language,
this is what is meant by the fruitful reception of a sacrament:
being present to the grace—the life—of Christ
by giving oneself over to the meaning of the sacramental act.

Jeffrey M. Kemper, *On the Table, At the Table,* 23.3 [1997]

SACRAMENT

The sacrifice of the cross and its sacramental renewal in the
Mass are one and the same. [GIRM 2]

*W*hen talking of sacraments,
it is perhaps better to use descriptions
rather than definitions.
Descriptions tend to engage our imaginations
more than do the usually sober definitions of sign,
institution and grace.
For example, here is how T.S. Eliot once described his craft:

Poetry is not the assertion that something is true,
but the making of that truth more real to us.

*A*ppropriating Eliot's description of poetry to describe
the sacraments,
we could say: The sacraments are not rituals
that merely assert that something is true . . .
they are ritual's visible words, *to use Augustine's phrase—*
that make the truth we profess more real to us.

*D*efinitions are essential to theology,
but they can limit us in ways we do not often realize.
How we define the sacraments is less important
than how the sacraments define us—
what the sacraments tell us about who we should be
and how we, as Christians who celebrate these rituals, should act.
The sacraments don't just tell us about the way;
as "visible words" they help us to commit ourselves to "do the way."

Kurt Stasiak, OSB, *Of Sacraments and Sacrifice*, 23.6 [1997]

SILENCE

Let All Mortal Flesh Keep Silence . . . [Ancient eucharistic hymn]

THE RISK OF SILENCE

*T*o bear silence is to risk disbelief.
    It is to chance the discovery
    that without our individual and collective artifacts,
    without our various kinds of noise,
    there is *nothing*.

*T*o dare the encounter with silence
    is to face the possibility that death,
    the silence into which we all must eventually fall,
    is a true void.

*L*iturgical silence, in this light, is an act of faith.
    It is a symbolic repudiation of humanity's worst fear
    and an affirmation of the essential Christian instinct
    that even the ultimate and irreversible experience of silence
    —death itself—
    is not outside the realm of the living and life-giving Word of God.

*V*erbosity in the liturgy can prevent the assembled believers
    from ever giving concrete expression to this trust
    upon which their unity is presumably founded.

*W*ords can become a smoke screen
    to shield us from our fear and doubt. . . .

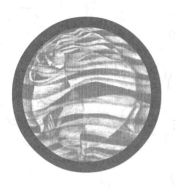

Silence in the liturgy
is a symbol of our willingness
to come face-to-face with the real God,
showing ourselves stripped of artifice and shield,
making ourselves known for who we truly are.
It is a response to the Christian's vocation to serve God
in spirit and truth.

Patrick Malloy, *In Search of Silence*, 18.2 [1992]

THE GROUND
FROM WHICH WORDS EMERGE

Silence is more than mere absence of noise,
or suspension of speech or a pause from activity.
In its fullest sense, it is less of a space between utterances,
than the very context and depth of utterances.
St. Ignatius of Antioch speaks of the Word
proceeding from the eternal silence of God,
just as the weighed and chosen words
of human utterance come from the deeper
recesses of our inner silence.

As the human word is not to be identified with chatter,
so human silence is more than absence of speech.
Rather it is the ground
from which the word emerges,
the home to which it returns.

In this sense, human silence and human speech
both model and reflect the deep silence of God
and the efficacy of God's eternal Word.

*I*t is from the silence, paradoxically,
that the word derives its power, its depth, its import;
and it is in the silence of the hearer's heart
that it finds its proper soil.
For words that ultimately matter, like God's own Word,
    stretch and strain to speak of that
      which lies too deep for words,
        and succeed only to the extent to which
        they fall into the ground and die.
        Speech must die to serve that which is spoken,
        says Paul Ricoeur.

        Mark Searle, *Silence,* Editorial, 9.1 [1982]

THE SILENCE OF CENTERING

*T*here is a necessary exercise of silence
    in which the participants,
    as individuals and as congregation,
"center" themselves, allow the inner noise to settle
and prepare to put down roots into the deep Self.
Very often, such an exercise is conceived of in highly individualistic terms,
which would seem to run counter to the communal character of our worship:
as if each of us is withdrawing beneath an invisible cowl of private introversion.

*T*here is a place for such interior withdrawal,
but it is not the liturgy of the church.
Liturgical silence as a centering exercise means a shared silence.
Max Picard speaks of the individual and the community
not standing against each other, but facing the silence together.

$\mathscr{Y}$et there is more to liturgical silence, even, than that.

> In liturgical silence it is the Body which centers itself in the silence,
> enters into the silence to become aware of itself
> precisely as Body animated by the one Spirit.
> We dwell in the silence *together* . . .
> a primary skill of liturgical participation
> which engenders the indispensable awareness
> that the Body of Christ, united with its Head,
> is more than just the sum of its parts.

Mark Searle, *Silence*, Editorial, 9.1 [1982]

THE SILENCE OF COMMUNION

$\mathscr{T}$here can be something uncomfortable, even dreadful,
about silence, especially the silence of God.
The silence of God is never broken:
it is only transformed.
It is transformed by God's love
into the Word that acts,
the action that speaks volumes.
But such Word-that-is-act seeks communion
where it might bear fruit.
The church itself is such a word;
so is the sacramental or ritual gesture;
so is the Word proclaimed.
All invite the silence of communion.

$\mathscr{A}$fter hearing the Word, or engaging in a rite,
or while being together with the faithful,
silence breeds awareness of the mystery.

There is also a kind of watching which is a silent communing;
a way of observing a ritual which respects it rather than inspects it,
which is a seeing with the mind's eye or with the eye of the heart.
Such silence is meditation, rumination, entering into the mystery, contemplating
sound and sign till they crack and open and yield their secret:
the presence of the sacred, of the powerful,
of a reality that overwhelms us in love.

Mark Searle, *Silence*, Editorial, 9.1 [1982]

THE SILENCE OF AWE

This kind of silence is the fruit of the others.
Theirs is the discipline which opens us to the divine gift:
its coming is beyond our manipulation,
beyond our power to produce . . .
and beyond our telling.

It leaves us speechless,
clutching at words hopelessly inadequate:
Lord, it is good for us to be here,
Lord, have mercy, . . .
or sheer silence.

It is not the silence of facing the void,
but a silence of encountering Presence:
dreadful yet thankful,
joyful yet sober,
awesome yet somehow reassuring.
It is where the heart finds rest,
even as it shudders.

Mark Searle, *Silence*, Editorial, 9.1 [1982]

WORD

When the Scriptures are read in the Church, God . . . is speaking. [GIRM 9]

Christ, present in his own word, is proclaiming the Gospel. [GIRM 9]

*T*he Word of God is more than the Bible—
it includes all of God's self-revealing activity.
God creates by means of the Word:
> *God said, 'Let there be light,' and there was light* [Genesis 1.3].

*T*he utterance of God brings about the calls of Abraham,
Moses, Samuel and David,
and reveals the law and the covenant.
The prophets begin their proclamations
The word of the Lord came to me . . . [cf. Isaiah 1.2].
God's word—*dabar*—is laden with power
and, once uttered, has a lasting effect in history.

*I*n the New Testament, Jesus continues to preach God's word.
His own preaching is also described as the *Word of God* [Luke 5.1].
But the startling new revelation concerning this Word is found
in the prologue to the Gospel of John:
> *In the beginning was the Word and the Word was with God,*
> *and the Word was God!* [John 1.1]

WORD

After describing the active presence of the Word
in creating and giving life,
the evangelist declares,

The Word was made flesh
and pitched his tent among us. [John 1.14]

*T*he Word of God is now in our very midst!
   Jesus, the Word of God,
   the Self-revelation of God,
   audibly, visibly, tangibly in our very midst!
   The mystery of the Incarnate Word
   is the foundation of our reverence
   for the Bible as Word of God.
   The scriptures, especially
   when they are proclaimed
   in the midst of the believing assembly,
   are the presence of Christ in our midst.

Irene Nowell, OSB, *Acknowledging Christ's Presence in the Word*, 1.2 [1988]

The ability to pray in Christ and in the Spirit derives . . . from the faith with which we submit to the Word addressed to us in the Scriptures and in the sacraments.

For in the liturgy, it is not only we who speak in union with Christ to God, but God addresses us in Christ in words of judgment and consolation, of call and of graciousness.

The introductory rites of the liturgy are intended as a process of "incorporation," whereby a crowd becomes one body, one Spirit in Christ and empties itself entirely to be open and vulnerable to God's Word. That Word . . . plunging, if allowed, into the depths of the one Body, arises again as prayer.

In the liturgy, the eternal mystery of the one Word proceeding forever from God and returning to God in the unity of the Spirit continues to unfold but, in the course of history, by grace we are caught up into that movement, baptised in the name of the Father, the Son and the Spirit, to participate in the very life of God.

Liturgical participation is nothing more than historically rehearsed participation in the trinitarian life.

Mark Searle, *The Spirit of the Liturgy*, 13.5 [1987]